Richard Scarry's

What Do People Do All Day?

HarperCollins *Children's Books*

This is Busytown.
My, what a nice town!

Richard Scarry's
What Do People Do All Day?

a poet writing poems

an artist painting a picture

a story writer

a pretty model

a businessman

a photographer

a secretary

an operator

CAFE

THE NEWS

THE REMARKABLE BOOK SHOP
E. KRAMER, PROP.

ABC

a book printer

a newspaper editor

a saleslady

a janitor

wspaper porter

FINISH YOUR MEALS!

wrong way Roger

Chimney swe

dentist

doctor

eye doctor

dressmaker

beauty parlour

real estate office

music teacher

BANK

CHEMIST

DANCING SCHOOL

PRESCRIPTIONS

street cleaner

Some workers work indoors and some work outdoors. Some work up in the sky and some work underground.

manhole cover

water hydrant

manhole

wire cable

sewer

lampp

sewage pipe

to sewage plant

All kinds of pipes and wires are buried underground

a stuck truck

FIRE STATIO

RITZ MANSIONS

HARDWARE

window washer

laundress

BARBER SHOP

delivery boy

MOTOR CARS

Some workers always do their
work at the same place.

Others travel from place
to place to do their jobs.

car salesman

TELEPHONE
BOOTH

What does your Daddy do?
What does your Mummy do?

jack
hammer

TAXI

And what do YOU do?
Are you a good helper?

ditch digger

Everyone is a worker

Farmer Alfalfa

Blacksmith fox

Stitches the tailor   Grocer cat   Mummy   Huckle

How many workers are there here?
One, two, three, four, five, six. What do these workers do?

Hi Daddy!

Farmer Alfalfa grows all kinds of food.
He keeps some of it for his family.

He sells the rest to Grocer Cat
in exchange for money.
Grocer Cat will send the food
to other people in Busytown.

GROCERIES

potatoes

Today Alfalfa bought a new suit with some of the money he got from Grocer Cat. Stitches, the tailor, makes clothes. Alfalfa bought his new suit from Stitches.

Then Alfalfa went to Blacksmith Fox's shop. He had saved enough money to buy a new tractor. The new tractor will make his farm work easier. With it he will be able to grow more food than he could grow before. He also bought some presents for Mummy and his son, Alfred.

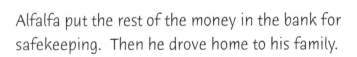

Alfalfa put the rest of the money in the bank for safekeeping. Then he drove home to his family.

Mummy loved her new earrings. Alfred loved his present, too.

What did the other workers do
with the money they earned?

First they bought food to eat and clothes to
wear. Then, they put some of the money in
the bank. Later they will use the money in
the bank to buy other things.

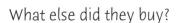

What else did they buy?

Stitches bought an egg beater so that his family could make fudge.
Try not to get any on your new clothes!

How do I look?

sand
bag

bellows

forge

Blacksmith Fox bought more iron for his shop.
He will heat and bend the metal to make more tractors and tools.

Grocer Cat bought a new dress for Mummy.
She earned it by taking such good care of the
house. He also bought a present for his son,
Huckle. Huckle was a very good helper today.

Mother's work is never done

Good Morning! Good Morning! The sun is up! Everybody up! Wash! Brush! Comb! Dress! Get up! There is a lot of work to be done!

Mummy and Sally and Harry made the beds.

They cleaned the house.

Mummy made sandwiches for lunch.

A brush salesman came to the door to sell
brushes. Mummy didn't want to buy
any brushes. My! He is trying very hard
to sell Mummy a brush of some kind, isn't he?

Daddy came home from work
and kissed everyone.

They sat down to supper.
Daddy should know better than to try to
take such a big bite.

After supper Mummy gave Sally and Harry a bath.

Daddy weighed himself on the scales.
I think he has eaten too much.

Daddy read a story before bedtime.

He climbed up to kiss Sally goodnight.
Oh dear! I just KNEW he had eaten too much!

Good Night!

Are you all right, Daddy?

I don't think anyone will ever
sleep in that bunk bed again.
Do you?

Sally and Harry had to sleep with Mummy. What would we ever
do if we didn't have mummies to do things for us all day – and
sometimes all night? Good night! Sleep tight!

A voyage on a ship

Captain Salty and his Crew are getting their ship ready for a voyage.
The ship will carry passengers to visit their friends in a faraway land across the ocean.

At last the ship is loaded with the food and
other things they will need on the long trip.
Here come the passengers!

gangplank

They have all bought tickets for the trip. They give the
tickets to the purser before they can go aboard the ship.
NO PUSHING PLEASE!

light buoy

7

TOOOOOOOOOOOt!
It is sailing time. A tiny tugboat pushes the big ocean liner away
from the pier. *Bon voyage!* The big ship sails out of the harbour.

Soon it is crossing the wide ocean.
There is no land in sight. Just look at all the
things that happen on an ocean-going ship!

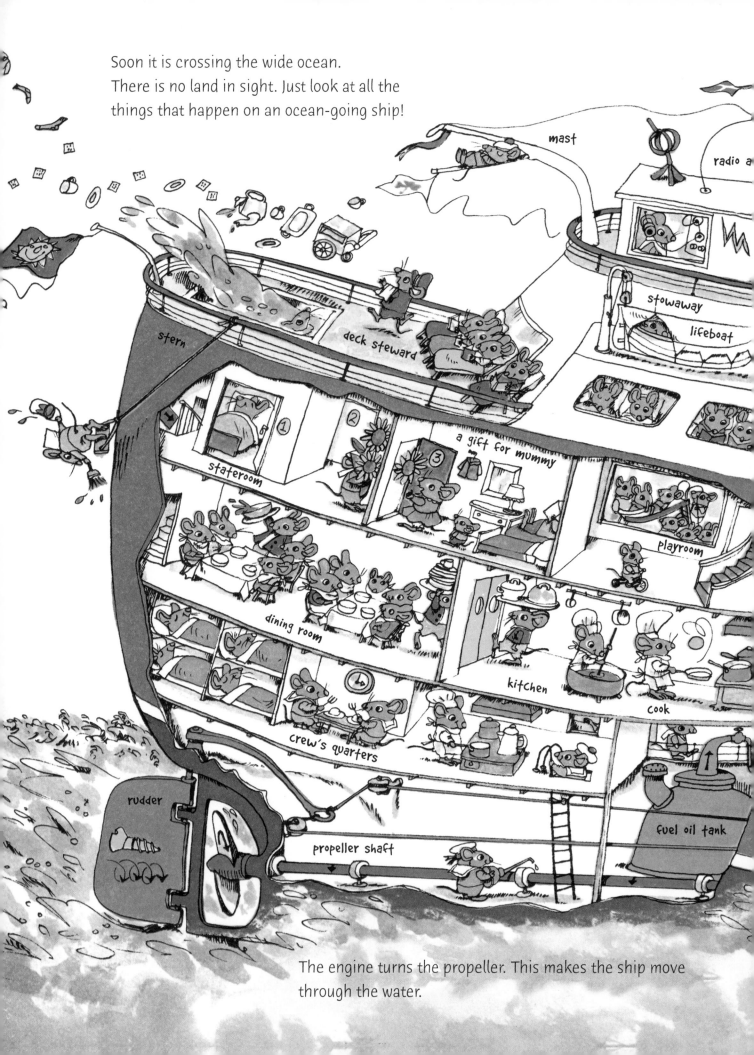

mast

radio a

stowaway

lifeboat

stern

deck steward

stateroom

a gift for mummy

playroom

dining room

kitchen

cook

crew's quarters

rudder

propeller shaft

fuel oil tank

The engine turns the propeller. This makes the ship move
through the water.

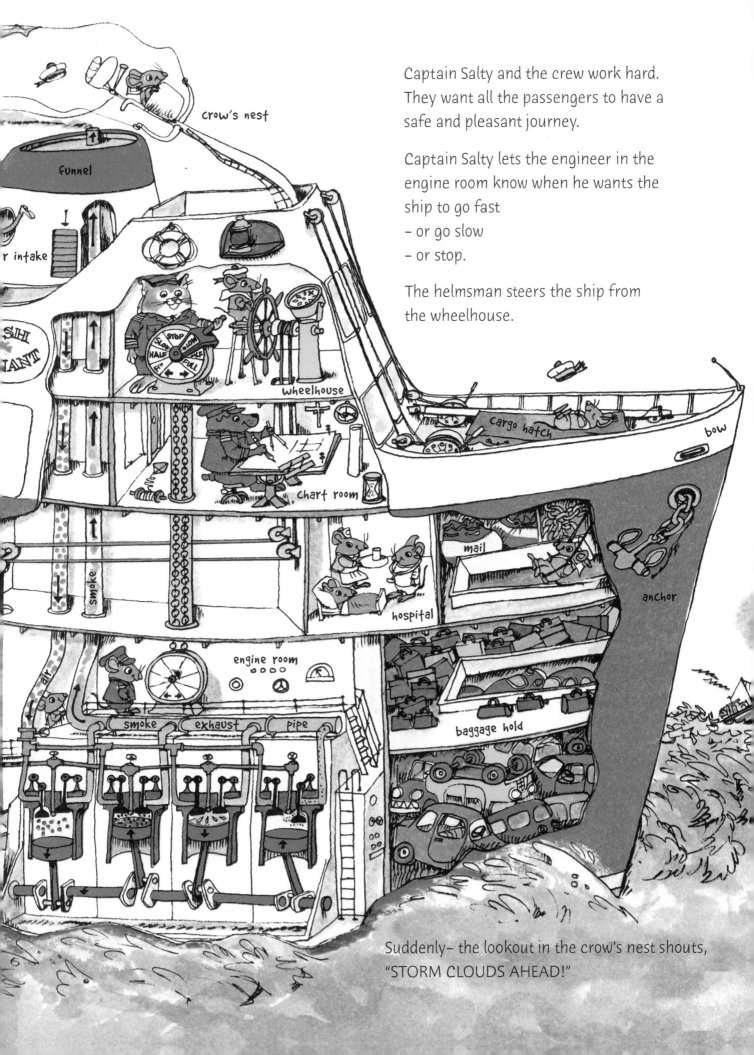

crow's nest

funnel

r intake

SH
ANT

wheelhouse

Captain Salty and the crew work hard.
They want all the passengers to have a
safe and pleasant journey.

Captain Salty lets the engineer in the
engine room know when he wants the
ship to go fast
– or go slow
– or stop.

The helmsman steers the ship from
the wheelhouse.

chart room

cargo hatch

bow

mail

hospital

anchor

smoke

engine room

air

smoke   exhaust   pipe

baggage hold

Suddenly- the lookout in the crow's nest shouts,
"STORM CLOUDS AHEAD!"

The storm hits the ship with great fury!
The radio operator hears someone calling on the radio.
"SOS! HELP! SAVE US! OUR BOAT IS SINKING!"

Look! There it is! It's a small fishing boat in trouble!

"FULL SPEED AHEAD!"
roars Captain Salty.
My, the sea is rough!

LOWER THE LIFEBOAT!
Hurry! Hurry! The fishing boat is sinking
Sailors Miff and Mo row to the rescue.

The boat sinks, but the fishermen are safe.

porthole

It's delicious!

Land Ho!!!

Back on board the liner, Captain Salty gives a party to celebrate the rescue. Will the storm never stop?

Then, just as suddenly as it started, the storm is over and the sea is calm. The ship continues on its journey.

Land ho! They have reached the other side of the ocean!

Everyone thanks the captain and crew for such an exciting voyage. Then they go ashore to visit friends. Other people have been waiting to cross the ocean to visit friends in Busytown. I wonder if their voyage will be as exciting as this one was?

No pushing please!

Policemen are working at all times to keep things safe and peaceful. When Sergeant Murphy is sleeping, Policeman Louie is awake. He will protect the townspeople from harm.

Good Morning!

Sleep tight!

In the morning, Officer Louie goes home to bed and Sergeant Murphy gets up. Now Sergeant Murphy will watch out for everyone's safety.

At the Police Station the police chief tells Murphy to drive around town on his motorcycle. The chief can talk to Murphy over the radio if he has something important to tell him.

radio room

Keep everything peaceful!

chief

HELP! HELP!
My little Huckle
is drowning!

First, Murphy saves Huckle from drowning in the fountain..

Be peaceful!

Then he has to stop two bad boys from fighting.
Look Murphy! There are two more!

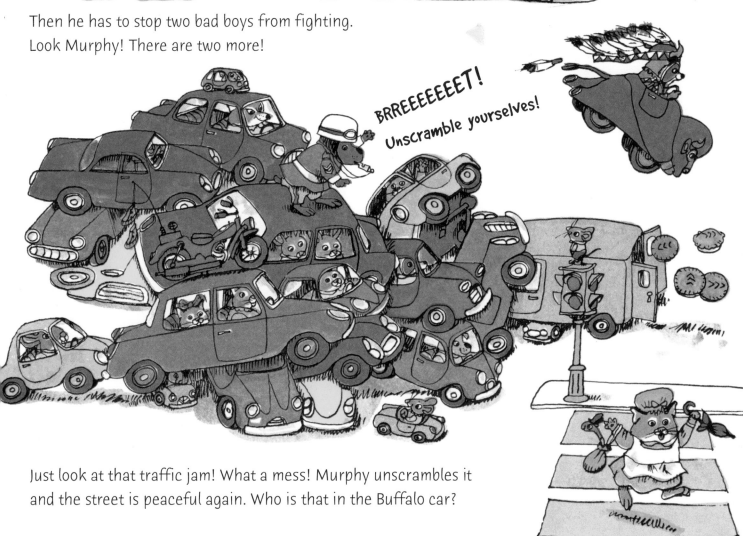

BRREEEEEEET!
Unscramble yourselves!

Just look at that traffic jam! What a mess! Murphy unscrambles it
and the street is peaceful again. Who is that in the Buffalo car?

O Ho! Wild Bill Hiccup and his Buffalomobile! He's speeding again!

He puts parking tickets on cars that are parked where they are not supposed to be.

Did you see that speeder hit Murphy's motorcycle? Chase him, Murphy!

Try to be good!

Murphy gives him a speeding ticket. For punishment he will not be allowed to drive his Buffalomobile for a few days. Let that be a lesson to you, Wild Bill Hiccup!

Now – guess what?
Grocer Cat telephones the Police Station.
A robber has stolen some bananas from the grocery store.

The chief of police calls Murphy over the radio. "CATCH THE THIEF!" he says.

Look Murphy! There's the thief now!
It's Gorilla Bananas!

Murphy chases after him.
OOPS! His motorcycle slipped on
a banana peel. It is good that he is
wearing a crash helmet.

He has captured Bananas!

The police van comes to take Bananas to jail.
He will stay there until he learns that it is
wrong to steal things from others.

It is time for Murphy to stop working. Now he can go home for supper with his family. Policeman Louie wakes up. He will keep everything peaceful during the night.

In the middle of the night, Louie hears a loud crying noise. If the noise doesn't stop it will wake up everyone in town. Why, it is Bridget, Murphy's little girl!
WAKE UP, MURPHY! BRIDGET IS HUNGRY!

Murphy has to get up and warm a bottle of milk for Bridget. Bridget stops crying.

Sergeant Murphy really knows how to keep Busytown safe and peaceful. Doesn't he?

Firemen to the rescue

FIRE!
Mother Cat was ironing one of Daddy's shirts. The iron was too hot. The shirt began to burn. "FIRE!" she shouted.

Davy Dog went to the Fire-alarm Box. He pulled the knob that sounded the alarm at the fire station.

LOCATION OF
ALARM BOXES

Hurry!

Firemen are at the fire station at all times. They have to be ready to put fires out quickly.

As soon as the alarm rang, they ran to their fire engines. HURRY!

Clang! Clang! Clang!
The firemen rushed to the fire.
They raised the ladder on the ladder
truck. A fireman ran up the ladder to
rescue Mummy. "SAVE MY HUCKLE!"
she screamed.

RESCUE-10

ALARM BOX

pumper engine

water hydrant

CHIEF

CHIEF

Save Huck too

Water is used to put fires out. The water runs through the pipes under the street.
The firemen attached a hose between the water hydrant and the pumper engine.
The pumper engine got water from the hydrant and squirted it out through the
hose nozzle.

But the ladder wasn't long
enough to reach Huckle up
in the playroom!
How will they ever save him?

"SAVE MY HUCKLE!" screamed Mummy Cat as the firemen carried her down.

Smokey came running to the house.
He had a smoke mask so that he would be able to breathe in the smoke-filled house.

He also had a special ladder.

He climbed up the fire-truck ladder as far as he could. He reached up with his special ladder and hooked it over the window sill. Then he climbed up. He just had to rescue Huckle!

The playroom door was closed. Smokey chopped it down with his axe.

He picked up Huckle – and he jumped out the window!

PLOPP!
Sparky and Snozzle were ready just in time to catch them in the life net. Daddy arrived just in time to see Smokey save Huckle.

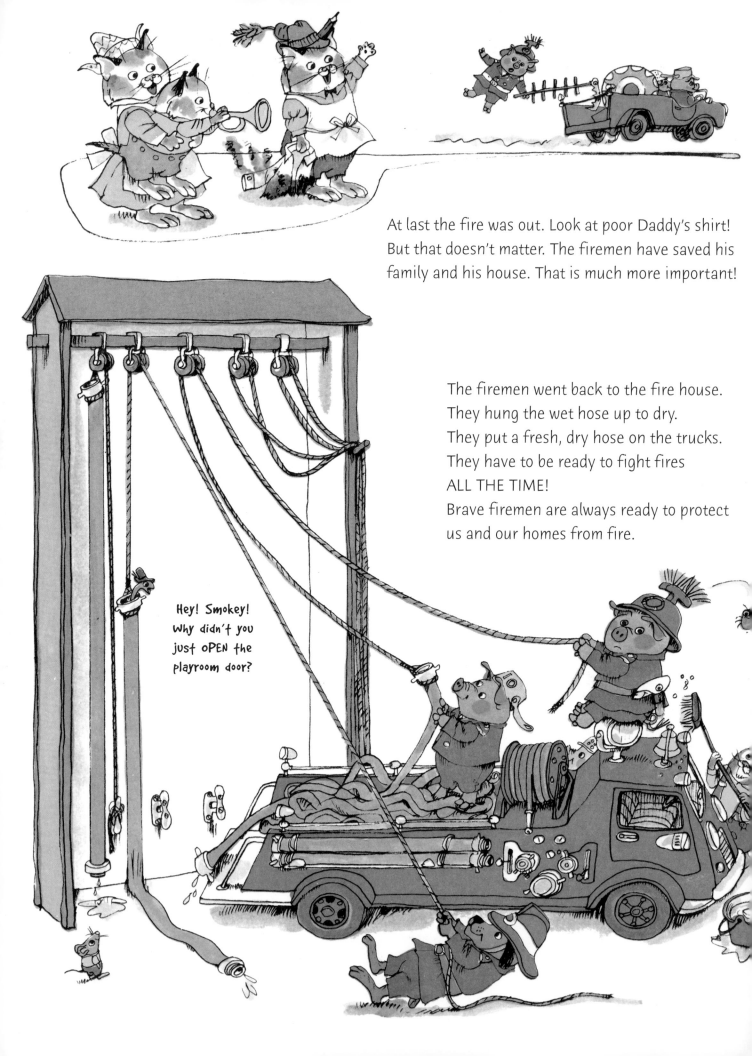

At last the fire was out. Look at poor Daddy's shirt! But that doesn't matter. The firemen have saved his family and his house. That is much more important!

The firemen went back to the fire house. They hung the wet hose up to dry. They put a fresh, dry hose on the trucks. They have to be ready to fight fires ALL THE TIME! Brave firemen are always ready to protect us and our homes from fire.

Hey! Smokey! Why didn't you just OPEN the playroom door?

A visit to the hospital

Mummy took Abby to visit Doctor Lion. He looked at her tonsils. "Hmmmm. Very bad tonsils," he said. "I shall have to take them out. Meet me at the hospital tomorrow."

On the next day, Daddy drove them to the hospital. Abby waved to the ambulance driver. Ambulances bring people to hospitals if they have to get there in a hurry.

Nurse Nelly was waiting for Abby. Mummy had to go home, but she promised to bring Abby a present after the doctor had taken her tonsils out.

Nurse Nelly took Abby up to the children's room.

Roger Dog was in the bed next to hers. His tonsils were already out. He was eating a big dish of ice cream.

Nurse Nelly put Abby on the bed. She pulled a curtain around them. No one could see what was going on

Why, she was helping Abby put on a nightgown!

Doctor Lion peeked into the room. He told Nurse Nelly he was going to put on his operating clothes. He told Nurse Nelly to bring Abby to the operating room.

Off to the operating room they went.
Doctor Lion was waiting there. Everyone but the patient wears a face mask in the operating room so that germs won't spread.

Doctor Lion told Abby that she was going to go to sleep. He said she would stay asleep until her tonsils were out.

Doctor Dog put a mask over her nose and mouth. She breathed in and out. In an instant she was asleep.

When she woke up she found herself back in the bed next to Roger's. Her tonsils were all gone! Her throat was sore, but it felt better after she had some ice cream.

whooooeeee!

Abby saw her Mummy arriving in the ambulance. Abby thought her mother must be in a hurry to see her.

Hurry!

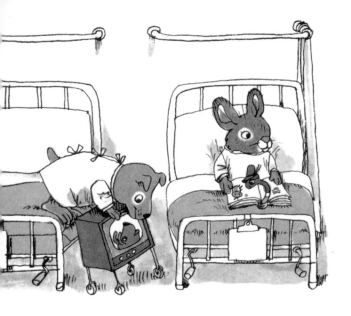

She waited and waited – but Mummy didn't come. At last Doctor Lion came. "Your Mother has brought you a present," he said. He took Abby for a ride in a wheelchair.

"There is your present," he said. "It is your new baby brother! Your Mother just gave birth to him here in the hospital." Then they all went to Mummy's room in the hospital. Daddy was there, too.

He looks like me, don't you think?

What a lucky girl she was! She left her tonsils at the hospital, but she brought home a lovely baby brother. But remember! Very few children receive such a nice present when they have their tonsils out!

The train trip

The Pig family is going on a train to visit their cousins in a town far away. They will travel all day and all night to get there.

Daddy buys train tickets at the railway station.

Mummy buys books and magazines to read.

A porter takes their bags to the train.

This old train has a steam engine.
It is only going to make a short trip to the next town.
The Pig family will ride overnight on another train.

wait! HALT!

Their train has a sleeping car with separate rooms for each family. These rooms are called compartments. At night, the seats will be made into beds. Look! There is Huckle's family.

Food and water is brought to the kitchen in the dining car. The cook will cook their meals. The waiter will serve them.

ALL ABOOOOOARD!
It is time to leave. The train rolls out of the station. The signal light tells the engineer that there is a clear track ahead. He doesn't want to bump into another train.

signal tower

COMING SOON

Mailbags and heavy baggage are put on the train. Some of it will be delivered to stations along the way.

The locomotive needs fuel oil to make its motors go. The motors turn the wheels so that the train can roll along the railway track.

The switchman can switch the train from one track to another. If he makes a mistake the train won't go to the right place.

The ticket collector takes the tickets. The tickets show that Daddy has paid for the trip.

In Huckle's compartment, the porter is getting the pillows and blankets ready for bedtime.

It is time to eat dinner. Cookie has already made the soup. He is trying to toss the pancakes from the side that is cooked to the side that is not cooked. You are not doing very well, Cookie!

The postman delivers a bag of mail to the railway station of a town they are passing through.

The watchman lowers the crossing gates before a train crosses a road. He doesn't want any cars to bump into the train. But Wild Bill Hiccup just HAS to bump into something!

Oh dear! The train has swerved and the waiter has spilled the soup!

While they are eating, the porter changes their seats into beds.

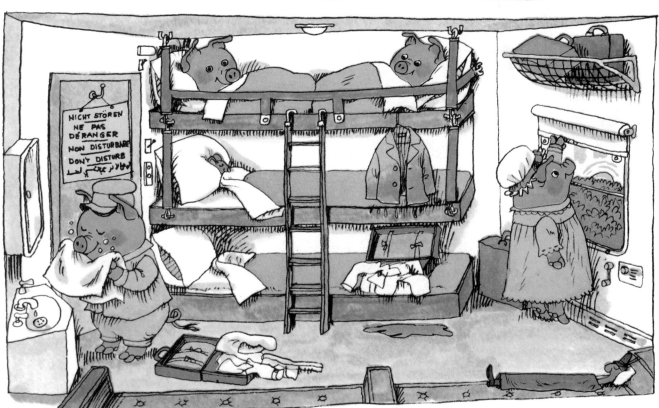

After dinner, everyone gets ready for bed.

Clickety clack, clickety clack.
The train speeds on through the night. The train crew won't go to sleep until the trip is over. Cookie is still trying to learn how to toss pancakes. Keep trying, Cookie.

WIENER SCHNITZEL

SLEEPING CAR

DINING CAR

It is morning when they arrive at their cousin's town. Their cousins are at the railway station to greet them.
I think they will have fun on their visit.
Don't you?

Wood and how we use it

We couldn't live without trees. We get wood from trees. We use wood in many ways. Let's see how we get our wood.

timber!

The lumberjack cuts down the tree.

The branches are cut off the tree trunk.

The tree trunk is sawed into logs.

tree trunk

a seed

a one year old tree

log

This tree is almost 100 years old and is ready to be cut down.

The logs are put in a river to float downstream.

The forest ranger watches out for fires. A forest fire could burn down a whole forest.

Some trees are left standing. Seeds from these trees will fall to the ground. New trees will grow in place of the old ones that have been cut down.

The foresters also scatter seeds from helicopters.

Loggers ride the logs down the river. They try to keep the logs from getting jammed. Oh dear! The logs are jammed! Unscramble that log jam, loggers!

Good work, loggers!
You broke up the log jam. Now the logs can float to the sawmill and be sawed into boards.

TOM SAWYER'S SAWMILL

Water falling over a water wheel makes all the machinery work.

timber

timberyard

SAWDUST THE CARPENTER

BOAT BUILDER

FURNITURE

he logs are sawed to rough boards.

The rough wood is sawed into boards of different sizes.

scrap timber

FOOLSCAP PAPER CO.

straddle truck

This timber is stacked in the timberyard to dry. Many kinds of workers come to buy the timber they need for building things. Daddy pig has bought some timber to build a bookcase.

The paper makers use scraps of wood to make paper.

FOOLSCAP PAPER COMPANY

chipper

blower

digester

chemicals

beater

mixer

Wet wood pulp moves onto a wire screen belt. Water is removed by rollers and dryers.

dry end   drying   paper making machine   wire screen   wet end   wet wood pulp

a finished roll of paper

ABC PRINTERS

Some paper is used to make bags and boxes.
Some is for making books. The paper used in this book
was taken to the printing shop where books are made.
The printer put the words and pictures on the pages.

The boat builder uses curved
pieces of wood to make boats.

BOAT BUILDER

FURNITURE MAKER

lathe

FURNITURE

SAWDUST THE CARPENTER

The furniture maker makes beds and chests and chairs.

Carpenters have a custom of nailing a tree branch to the roof of a new house.

Some trees give us fruit.

POLLY   JAN

MA   PA

D.S.   D.C.

NEWS
Great Plumbing and Heating Problems at the Retan house. More later.

ICE CREAM

Harry is planting an apple seed. An apple tree will grow from the seed. It will take a long time. Someday YOU might like to plant a tree.

Trees shade us from the hot sun.

Digging coal to make electricity work for us

steam boiler

STOP GO

FRESH AIR ENTER HERE

Pick! Pick! Pick! Dig! Dig! Dig! The miners dig coal out of the coal mine under the ground.

Water seeps into the mine, and has to be pumped out.

Lifts raise and lower the miners and coal cars.

After the coal is dug out, wooden props are needed to hold up the roof.

The miners use picks and drills to break the coal into small pieces.

The seeping water collects in the sump.

sump

Many years ago, sunlight poured down on the plants and trees and helped them to grow. When these plants and trees died, they sank into the ground. Gradually they were changed into coal.

BURIED SUNLIGHT COAL MINE

THE TIPPLE

COAL

COAL

DIANE

The coal is brought up out of the mine to the tipple. Then it is loaded into railway coal cars.

Miners need fresh air. A fan blows out the stale air and fresh air rushes in.

The miners blast the hard, black coal with explosives.

EXPLOSIVE

stale air leaves this way

The loader loads coal into small coal cars.

TO THE TIPPLE

loader

By burning coal, we are able to make electricity work for us.
The electricity lights our homes. That is why we call coal "buried
sunlight." There is electricity in everything. But it is not useful to
us until it is moving. Coal helps to make electricity move.

A train brings the
coal to the electric
power plant.

LET
THERE
BE
LIGHT

ELECTRIC POWER PLANT

water

steam

It's hot
in here!

fan

boiler room

boiler

The coal is burned in the boiler to heat water.
The heat turns the water into steam.
The boiler works like a tea kettle.

PLEASE
EMPTY
COAL CARS
HERE

COAL

COAL

DIANE

STOP

to open   to close

a lazy fellow

The steam forces the turbine to turn, just as the wind moves a windmill. This turbine turns the electric generator that forces the electricity to move. This moving electricity is called an electric current.

$$resistance = \frac{potential\ difference}{current}$$

OHM'S LAW

turbine

electric generator

the steam is cooled,

and condenses back to water

PUMP

The electric current travels through wires into our homes.

substation

Electricity is used in many ways. But the most important use of all is to give us light.

main switch

Building a new road

Good roads are very important to all of us. Doctors need them to visit patients. Firemen need them to go to fires. We all need them to visit one another. The road between Busytown and Workville was bumpy and crooked and very dusty –

–except when it rained!
Then the dirt turned to mud and everyone got stuck.

The mayors of the two towns went to the road engineer and
told him that they wanted to have a new road.
The townspeople had agreed to pay the road engineer and
his workers to build the new road.

Get rid of those bumps! Make this road flat and straight, Bugdozer!

surveying instrument.

ROAD PLANS

BUMP

The surveyor used his instruments to make sure that the road would be straight.

The motor crane lifts heavy things

The grader makes the ground smooth

The road builders used many machines to build roads. They put down big pipes to let streams of water flow under the road.

The bulldozer moves dirt

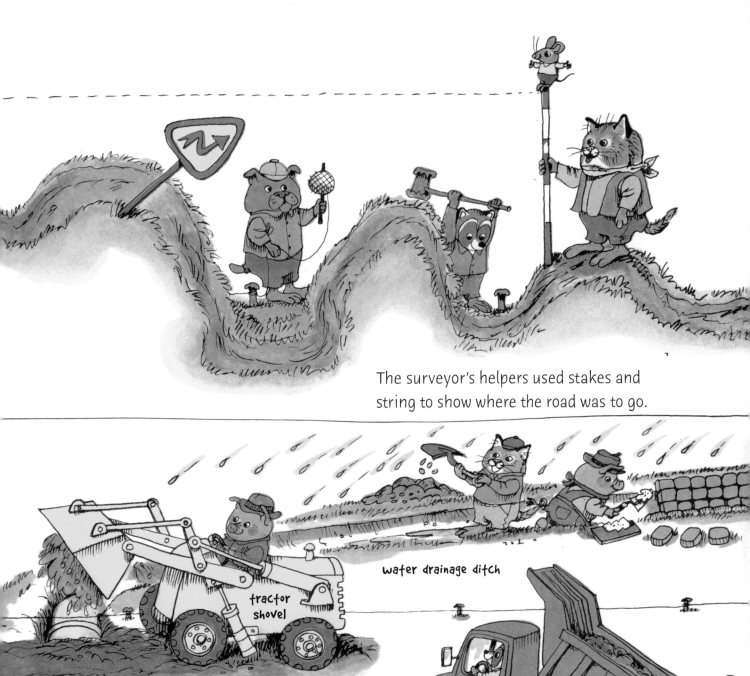

The surveyor's helpers used stakes and string to show where the road was to go.

water drainage ditch

tractor shovel

ditch digger

dump truck

At last the roadbed was straight and smooth. But it needed a hard top so that there would be no dust or mud.

power shovel

rock crusher

Big rocks were put into the rock crusher
to be crushed into smaller stones.

A stone spreader spread the
stones evenly over the roadbed.

ASPHALT OIL SPREADER

stone spreader

dump truck

A truck squirted sticky asphalt oil on the
stones to make them stick together.

keystone

The stone cuter shapes the stones
so that they will fit next to each other.

sand pile

bucket loader

hot asphalt mixer

TAR TAR

TAR

The asphalt mixer made hot, sticky asphalt.

dump truck

level finisher

roller

The asphalt was poured into the level finisher, which spread it out flat on the road.

A heavy roller pressed down the asphalt to make it smooth and hard.

A GOOD ROAD

How am I doing, chief?

The road was built high in the middle so that rain water would roll off into ditches at the sides.

Street lights were put up so that drive
could see the road clearly at night.

The workers put up guard rails to keep cars from going off the road.

They posted many signs. Some signs remind drivers to drive safely. Some signs show which way to go.

A dividing line painter painted a line down the middle of the road. Dividing lines remind drivers to keep on their own side.

Everyone wanted to be the first one to drive on the new road. But Grandma Cat was the first! Wasn't she lucky?

Water

We all need water. Nothing on earth can live without it. Even though we can't see it, there is a lot of water in the air. Sometimes it falls to earth as rain or snow. Then we can see it and feel it.

Now, let's see how we can make water work for us.

stream

water reservoir

water intake

dam

a picnic

ELECTRIC POWER STATION

electric generator

CROSS SECTION OF DAM

dam

A dam has been built across the river valley to hold the water back. After the water has been used in the electric power plant, it flows as a river down to the sea.

The wind turns the whirling vanes on the windmill. This causes buckets to lift water to feed the thirsty plants in the farm field up above the river.

Water lies in pools underground and can be pumped up for use.

river

The river water must be made clean and pure, so that it will be safe to drink. Water is pumped into the waterworks.

PUMPING STATION

pump

WATERWORKS PURIFICATION PLANT

lime   alum   soda ash

The chemists put chemicals in the water to kill harmful germs.

CHEMICAL HOUSE

CHEMICAL SUPPLY CO.

mixing tank

PUMPING STATION

filter

sand

gravel

steam engine

water intake

GERMS BEWARE!

chlorine kills germs

filtered water reservoir

centrifugal pump

river

The water is clean after it flows through the waterworks.
Then the water is pumped through underground pipes to everyone.

river bank

Water is used for many things. It gets dirty and must be made clean again at the sewage plant before it is put in the sea.

sun

cloud

water is delicious!

sewer gas vent

bathroom

The heat of the sun makes water return to the air. This rising water is called vapour. You cannot see water vapour, but one day it will again fall to earth as rain or snow.

I'll see you later water vapour!

sewage treatment plant

hot water heater

sink

clothes washer

stove

kitchen

water hydrant

sewer pipe

lighthouse

TO OTHER HOUSES

manhole cover

seawall

Boats use river and ocean waterways to carry people and cargo to other places.

And also – rivers and lakes and oceans are just nice to look at. Don't you think so?

you are now entering the ocean

this is the end of the river

HELP!

CLEOPATRA'S BARGE

seashore

First published in 1968
This edition published by HarperCollins Children's Books in 2010

HarperCollins Children's Books is a division of HarperCollins Publishers Ltd,
77-85 Fulham Palace Road, London W6 8JB

1 3 5 7 9 10 8 6 4 2

ISBN: 978-0-00-793518-5

The HarperCollins website address is www.harpercollins.co.uk

Printed in China by South China Printing Co. Ltd